**Managing Editor**
Ina Massler Levin, M.A.

**Editor**
Eric Migliaccio

**Contributing Editor**
Sarah Smith

**Creative Director**
Karen J. Goldfluss, M.S. Ed.

**Cover Design**
Tony Carrillo / Marilyn Goldberg

***Teacher Created Resources***
12621 Western Avenue
Garden Grove, CA 92841
www.teachercreated.com

**ISBN: 978-1-4206-5943-6**



Reprinted, 2026

Made in U.S.A.

# This book belongs to

______________________________

Ready·Set·Learn

# Get Ready to Learn!

Get ready, get set, and go! Boost your child's learning with this exciting series of books. Geared to help children practice and master many needed skills, the *Ready Set Learn* books are bursting with 64 pages of learning fun. Use these books for . . .

- enrichment
- skills reinforcement
- extra practice

With their smaller size, the *Ready Set Learn* books fit easily in children's hands, backpacks, and book bags. All your child needs to get started are pencils, crayons, and colored pencils.

A full sheet of colorful stickers is included. Use these stickers for . . .

- decorating pages
- rewarding outstanding effort
- keeping track of completed pages

Celebrate your child's progress by using these stickers on the reward chart located on the inside cover. The blue-ribbon sticker fits perfectly on the certificate on page 64.

With *Ready Set Learn* and a little encouragement, your child will be on the fast track to learning fun!

# Dog Search

**Directions:** Find and circle the words.

| | | | | | | |
|---|---|---|---|---|---|---|
| l | f | a | s | m | o | g |
| i | r | s | t | l | n | d |
| h | o | g | e | o | d | o |
| i | g | g | e | g | j | d |
| f | o | g | r | o | o | o |
| e | s | c | l | o | g | g |
| e | e | m | e | s | i | n |

**dog** **log** **jog** **clog**
**hog** **fog** **frog** **smog**

# Flying Word Search

**Directions:** Find and circle the words.

| | | | | | | | | |
|---|---|---|---|---|---|---|---|---|
| s | o | g | g | y | o | w | e | t |
| t | g | o | p | e | n | u | p | h |
| o | e | t | e | s | e | t | b | e |
| r | t | o | t | h | e | j | e | t |
| m | e | t | m | e | l | e | t | y |

| | | | |
|---|---|---|---|
| **jet** | **let** | **met** | **set** |
| **wet** | **pet** | **get** | **bet** |

# Bug Search

**Directions:** Find and circle the words.

| | | | |
|---|---|---|---|
| **bug** | **dug** | **hug** | **tug** |
| **rug** | **jug** | **plug** | **mug** |

# Fish Search

**Directions:** Find and circle the words.

| | | | | | | | |
|---|---|---|---|---|---|---|---|
| t | o | s | p | i | n | i | b |
| h | e | a | t | t | i | n | y |
| i | f | g | r | i | n | g | p |
| n | o | p | i | n | o | f | i |
| g | r | i | p | o | w | i | n |
| o | c | h | i | n | a | n | g |
| f | r | o | g | e | y | e | s |

| | | | |
|---|---|---|---|
| **fin** | **win** | **chin** | **grin** |
| **pin** | **tin** | **spin** | **thin** |

# "un" Words

**Directions:** Find and circle the "un" words. Use words from the word box.

| | | | | | | | | |
|---|---|---|---|---|---|---|---|---|
| j | s | u | m | v | u | n | o | p |
| u | t | u | b | l | a | s | f | u |
| s | u | n | o | n | e | p | l | m |
| t | n | u | t | o | r | u | n | p |
| a | o | b | u | n | a | n | u | t |
| n | r | u | b | i | n | f | u | n |

| | | |
|---|---|---|
| **sun** | **bun** | **stun** |
| **fun** | **run** | **spun** |

# Cap Search

**Directions:** Find and circle the "ap" words.

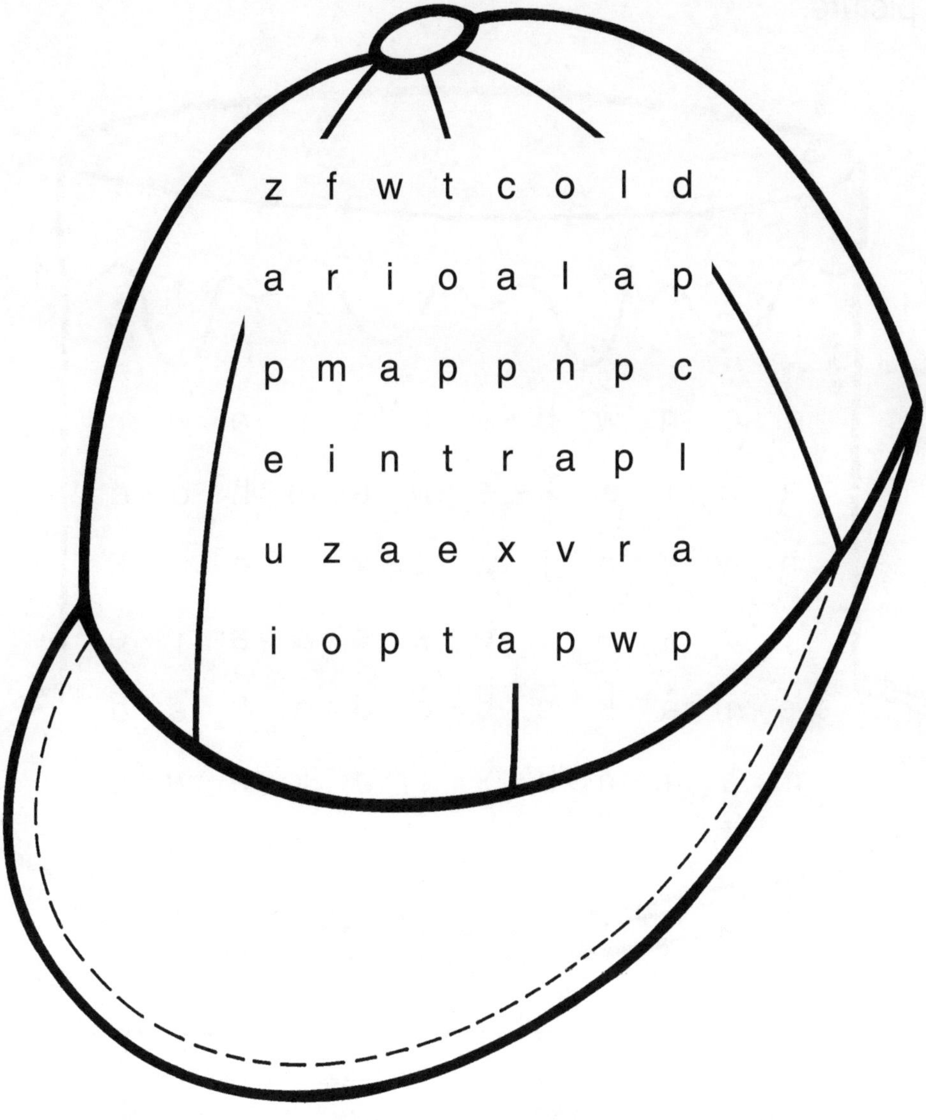


**lap** **tap** **trap** **map**
**nap** **clap** **cap** **zap**

# "ake" Words

**Directions:** Find and circle the "ake" words in the puzzle. Color the picture.

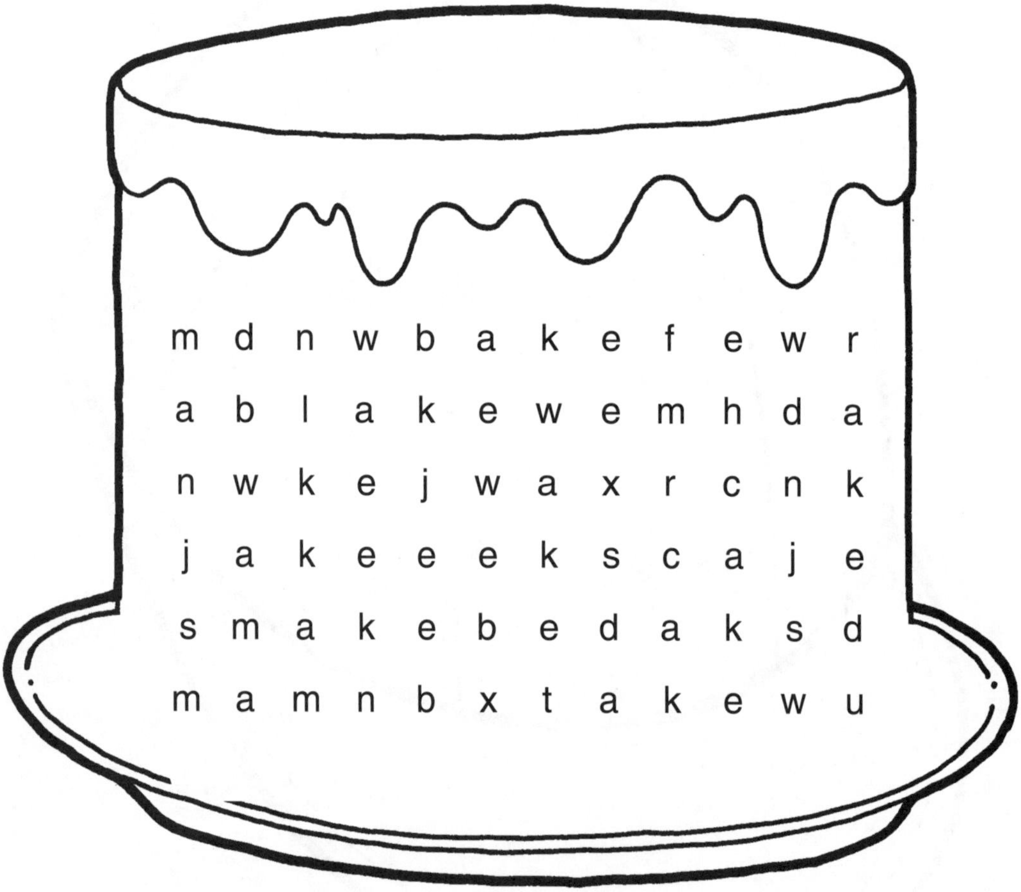

| | | | | | | | | | | | |
|---|---|---|---|---|---|---|---|---|---|---|---|
| m | d | n | w | b | a | k | e | f | e | w | r |
| a | b | l | a | k | e | w | e | m | h | d | a |
| n | w | k | e | j | w | a | x | r | c | n | k |
| j | a | k | e | e | e | k | s | c | a | j | e |
| s | m | a | k | e | b | e | d | a | k | s | d |
| m | a | m | n | b | x | t | a | k | e | w | u |

| | | | |
|---|---|---|---|
| **bake** | **cake** | **Jake** | **lake** |
| **make** | **rake** | **take** | **wake** |

# "ice" Words

**Directions:** Find and circle the "ice" words in the puzzle. Color the picture.

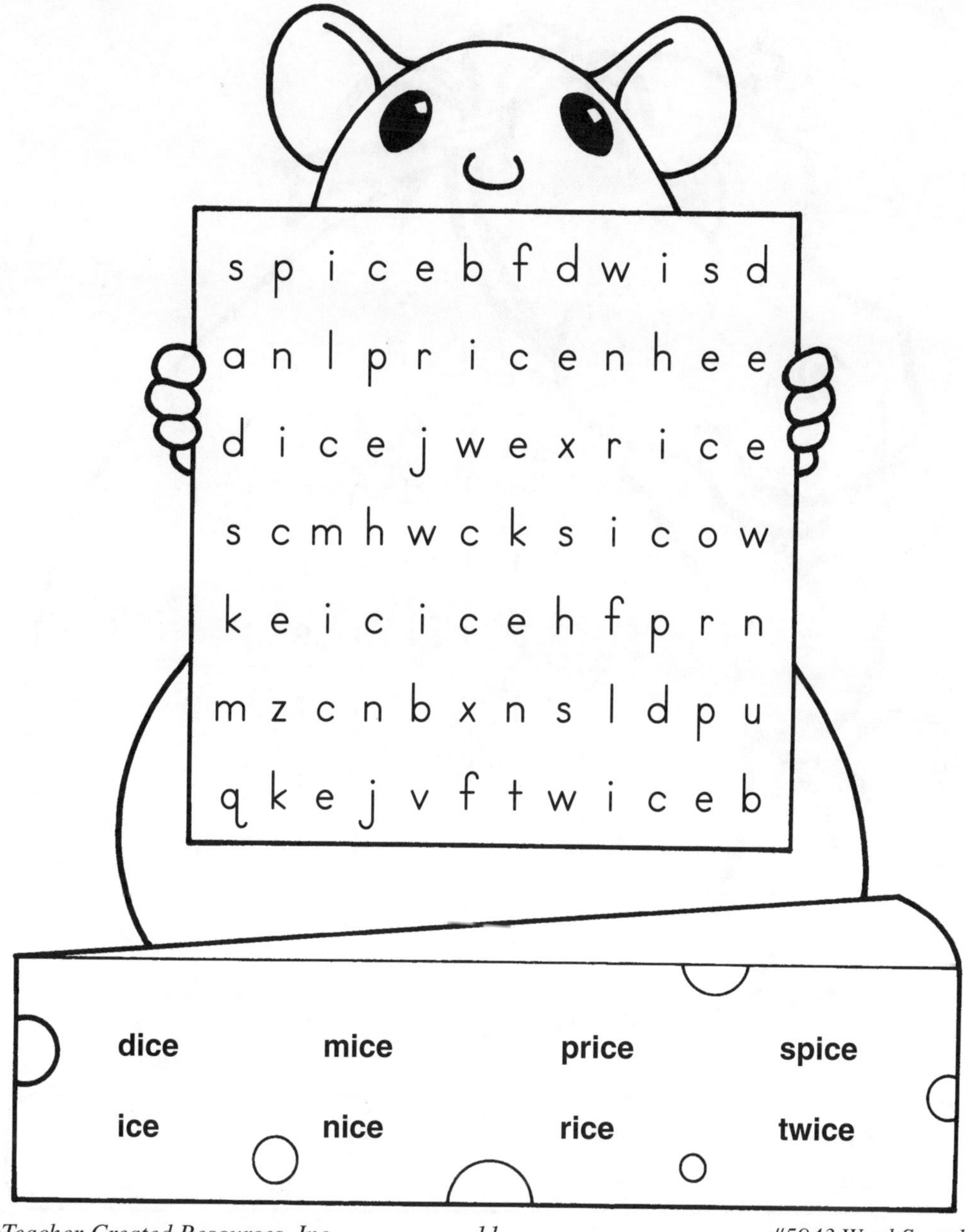

| | | | | | | | | | | | |
|---|---|---|---|---|---|---|---|---|---|---|---|
| s | p | i | c | e | b | f | d | w | i | s | d |
| a | n | l | p | r | i | c | e | n | h | e | e |
| d | i | c | e | j | w | e | x | r | i | c | e |
| s | c | m | h | w | c | k | s | i | c | o | w |
| k | e | i | c | i | c | e | h | f | p | r | n |
| m | z | c | n | b | x | n | s | l | d | p | u |
| q | k | e | j | v | f | t | w | i | c | e | b |

| | | | |
|---|---|---|---|
| **dice** | **mice** | **price** | **spice** |
| **ice** | **nice** | **rice** | **twice** |

# "it" Words

**Directions:** Find and circle the "it" words. Use the words in the word box.

s p o t b k m
w i d h e i r
n t o e s t i
s l i t s t i
g s f i t e p
i b a s i t p
h i t l i t e
e t r o b e d

| | | | |
|---|---|---|---|
| **fit** | **sit** | **bit** | **kit** |
| **pit** | **lit** | **hit** | **slit** |

 

# "ip" Words

**Directions:** Find and circle the "ip" words. Use the words in the word box below.

| | | | | | | | | | | |
|---|---|---|---|---|---|---|---|---|---|---|
| z | z | i | p | p | e | r | y | t | i | n |
| i | o | s | u | m | m | e | r | r | s | o |
| s | i | p | f | d | o | s | h | i | p | d |
| g | i | r | l | i | p | t | i | p | o | o |
| e | m | h | i | p | l | a | r | i | p | s |
| r | i | m | p | e | l | y | l | m | e | e |

| | | | | |
|---|---|---|---|---|
| **ship** | **dip** | **sip** | **flip** | **zip** |
| **rip** | **hip** | **tip** | **trip** | **lip** |

# "ee" Words

**Directions:** Circle the words with the "ee" sound.

| | | | | | | | | | |
|---|---|---|---|---|---|---|---|---|---|
| f | h | m | e | k | m | i | r | j | w |
| d | b | r | g | f | e | e | i | s | e |
| t | e | b | x | n | s | t | d | s | d |
| c | r | e | t | f | h | r | q | w | s |
| l | a | e | a | p | e | e | d | o | e |
| a | u | h | w | o | x | e | g | n | e |
| b | t | m | h | g | o | k | h | o | n |

**be** **me**
**bee** **see**
**fee** **tree**
**he** **we**

# "eep" Words

**Directions:** Circle the "eep" words. Color the picture.

| | | | | | | | | | | | |
|---|---|---|---|---|---|---|---|---|---|---|---|
| b | e | e | p | r | b | f | d | w | i | s | d |
| m | s | m | n | b | x | n | e | l | d | w | u |
| k | h | k | e | e | p | f | e | f | e | e | p |
| a | e | l | a | e | a | w | p | m | h | e | e |
| n | e | a | n | j | e | e | p | r | g | p | e |
| q | p | k | j | v | f | g | o | w | e | e | p |

| | | | |
|---|---|---|---|
| **beep** | **jeep** | **peep** | **sweep** |
| **deep** | **keep** | **sheep** | **weep** |

# "og" Words

**Directions:** Find and circle the "og" words.

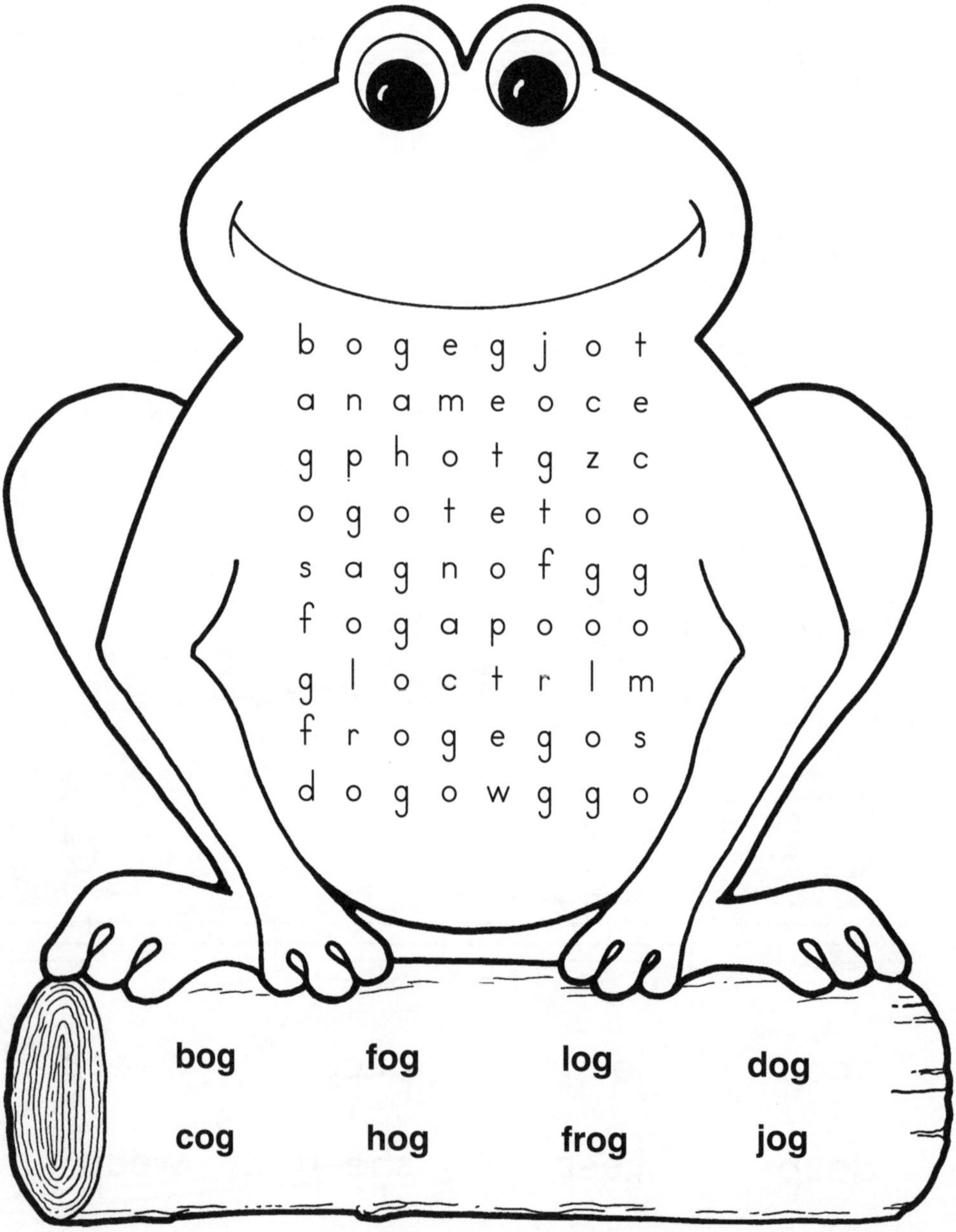

# "est" Words

**Directions:** Find and circle the "est" words. Use the words in the word box.

| | | | | | | | | |
|---|---|---|---|---|---|---|---|---|
| o | w | v | e | s | t | h | e | m |
| v | e | e | r | t | o | m | a | a |
| e | s | n | b | o | n | e | s | t |
| r | t | t | e | l | l | y | t | e |
| c | h | e | s | t | y | e | i | s |
| o | l | d | t | o | r | e | s | t |
| b | u | m | p | e | s | t | h | o |

| | | | |
|---|---|---|---|
| **best** | **rest** | **west** | **nest** |
| **vest** | **chest** | **test** | **pest** |

# "ock" Words

**Directions:** Circle the words in the puzzle. Color the picture.

dock
lock
rock
sock
block
clock
knock
shock

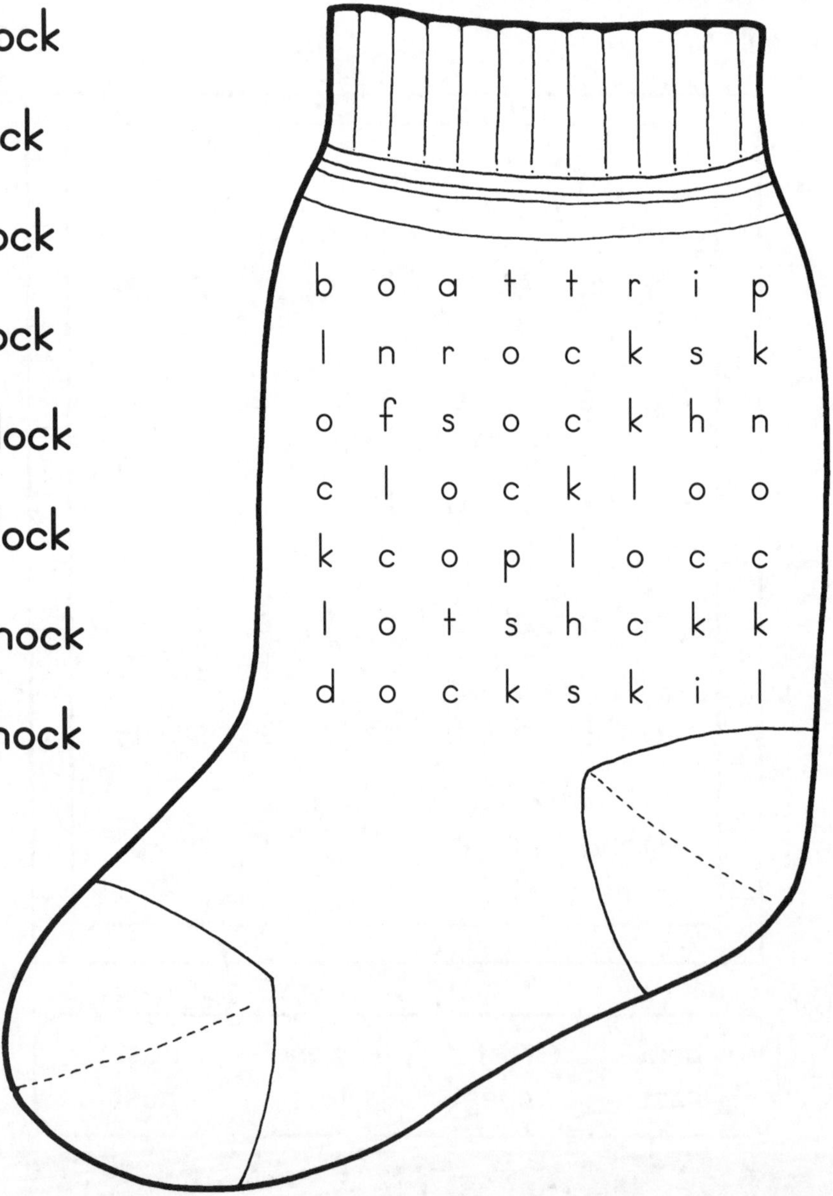

| | | | | | | | |
|---|---|---|---|---|---|---|---|
| b | o | a | t | t | r | i | p |
| l | n | r | o | c | k | s | k |
| o | f | s | o | c | k | h | n |
| c | l | o | c | k | l | o | o |
| k | c | o | p | l | o | c | c |
| l | o | t | s | h | c | k | k |
| d | o | c | k | s | k | i | l |

# "ine" Words

**Directions:** Circle the words in the puzzle. Color the picture.

w w a f i n e x r g n d

i s l a p n w p i n e s

n d f n w e k d i n e h

e m i n e b f d w i s i

m h m v b x b s l d s n

s d n w e o l i n e w e

q k v i n e g o k f k b

| | | | |
|---|---|---|---|
| dine | line | pine | vine |
| fine | mine | shine | wine |

# "eat" Words

**Directions:** Circle the words in the puzzle. Color the picture.

| | | | | | | | | | |
|---|---|---|---|---|---|---|---|---|---|
| d | f | h | w | h | e | a | t | r | j |
| d | t | r | e | a | t | h | f | e | r |
| t | m | e | j | w | o | e | r | a | n |
| m | d | n | r | b | m | a | t | i | e |
| z | r | e | a | t | e | t | l | d | a |
| k | d | h | v | f | a | o | k | f | t |
| s | e | a | t | a | t | b | e | a | t |

| | | | |
|---|---|---|---|
| beat | heat | neat | treat |
| eat | meat | seat | wheat |

# "old" Words

**Directions:** Circle the words in the puzzle. Color the picture.

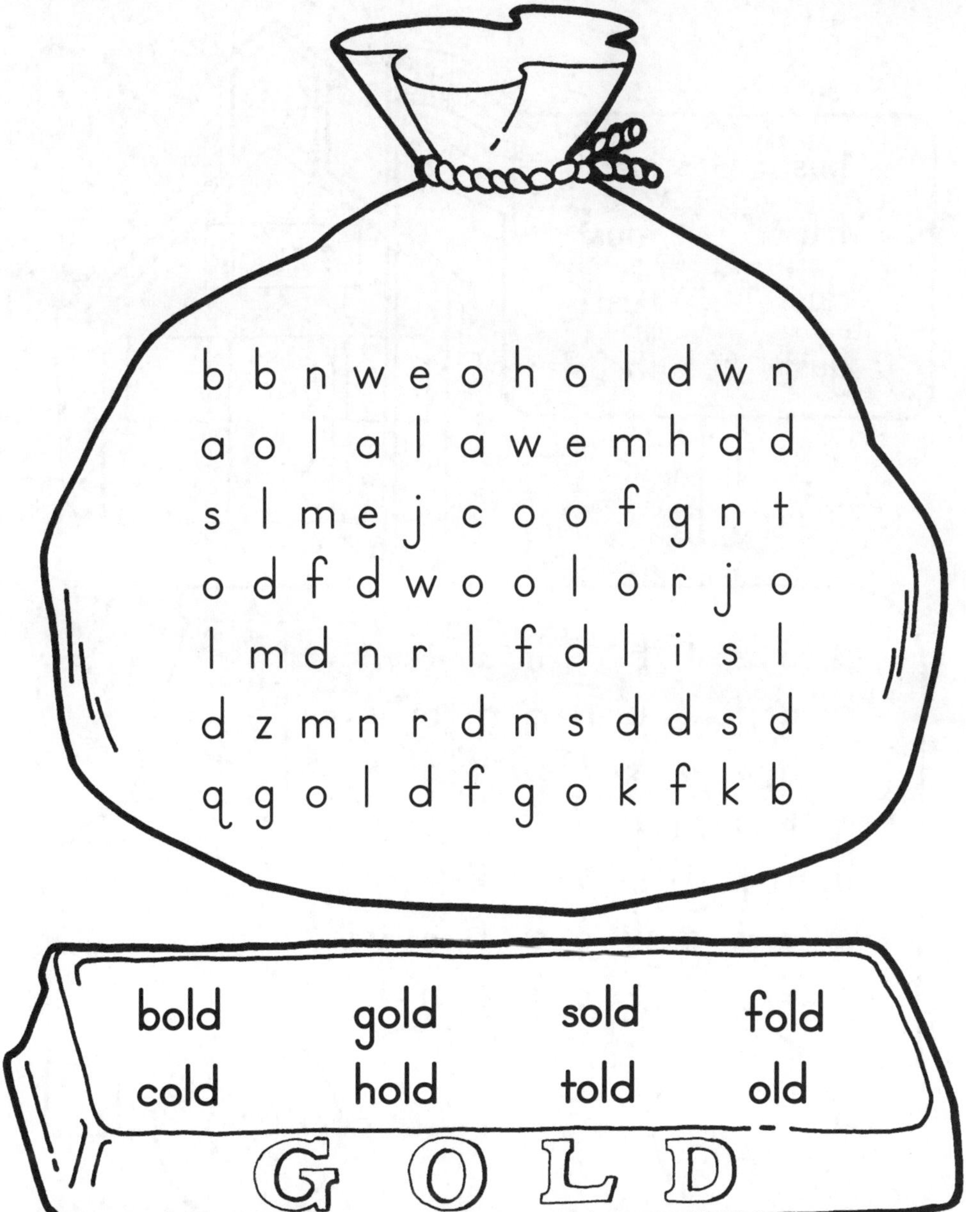


| | | | | | | | | | | | |
|---|---|---|---|---|---|---|---|---|---|---|---|
| b | b | n | w | e | o | h | o | l | d | w | n |
| a | o | l | a | l | a | w | e | m | h | d | d |
| s | l | m | e | j | c | o | o | f | g | n | t |
| o | d | f | d | w | o | o | l | o | r | j | o |
| l | m | d | n | r | l | f | d | l | i | s | l |
| d | z | m | n | r | d | n | s | d | d | s | d |
| q | g | o | l | d | f | g | o | k | f | k | b |

bold gold sold fold
cold hold told old

# "ust" Words

**Directions:** Circle the words in the puzzle. Color the picture.

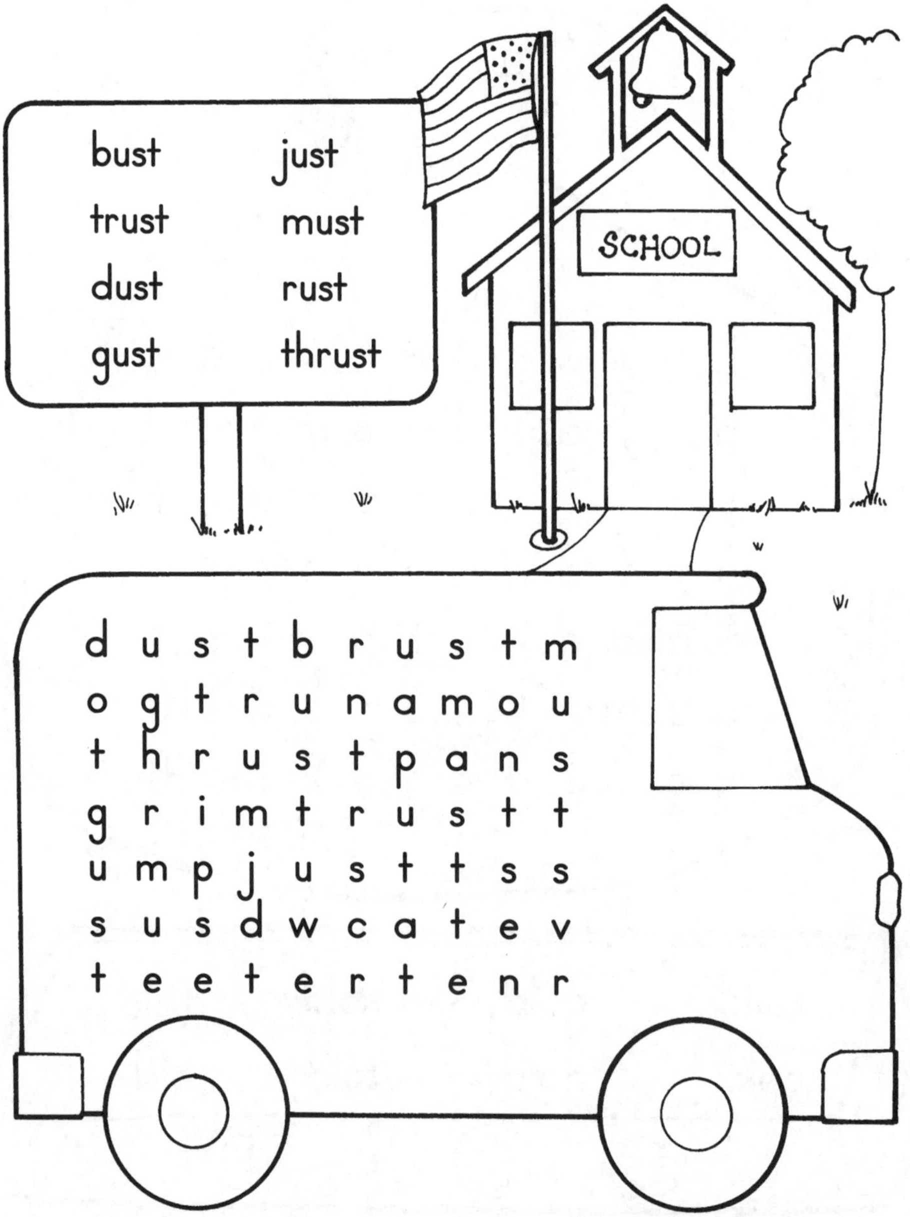


| | |
|---|---|
| bust | just |
| trust | must |
| dust | rust |
| gust | thrust |

| | | | | | | | | | |
|---|---|---|---|---|---|---|---|---|---|
| d | u | s | t | b | r | u | s | t | m |
| o | g | t | r | u | n | a | m | o | u |
| t | h | r | u | s | t | p | a | n | s |
| g | r | i | m | t | r | u | s | t | t |
| u | m | p | j | u | s | t | t | s | s |
| s | u | s | d | w | c | a | t | e | v |
| t | e | e | t | e | r | t | e | n | r |

 

Ready·Set·Learn

# "oke" Words

**Directions:** Circle the words in the puzzle. Color the picture.

| | | | | | | | | | | | |
|---|---|---|---|---|---|---|---|---|---|---|---|
| q | j | o | k | e | f | g | y | k | f | k | c |
| s | p | f | h | w | s | k | o | i | r | j | h |
| e | s | o | a | l | m | w | k | b | h | e | o |
| s | w | a | l | h | o | o | e | r | g | k | k |
| o | m | d | n | e | k | f | d | o | i | o | e |
| w | o | k | e | b | e | p | o | k | e | r | u |
| k | s | p | o | k | e | f | h | e | e | w | n |

poke joke yoke smoke
choke broke spoke woke

# "ight" Words

**Directions:** Circle the words in the puzzle. Color the picture.

```
k s n w e t i g h t w n
b s i g h t f e b h d i
r w l u j w i x r g n g
i r i g p t g s i m j h
g m g n r t h d g r s t
h z h n b x t s h b s u
t k t f m i g h t m k b
```

| | | | |
|---|---|---|---|
| bright | light | night | sight |
| fight | might | right | tight |

# Long "u" Words

**Directions:** Circle the words in the puzzle. Color the picture.

| | | | | | | | | | | | |
|---|---|---|---|---|---|---|---|---|---|---|---|
| s | d | s | u | i | t | k | s | i | r | f | w |
| s | m | d | e | r | b | f | t | i | o | r | f |
| m | z | x | n | b | x | l | s | l | d | u | u |
| k | u | n | w | e | o | u | h | f | e | i | n |
| c | u | t | e | l | a | t | e | m | h | t | e |
| n | w | a | e | j | w | e | x | r | g | n | d |
| q | k | d | j | v | f | g | o | m | u | t | e |

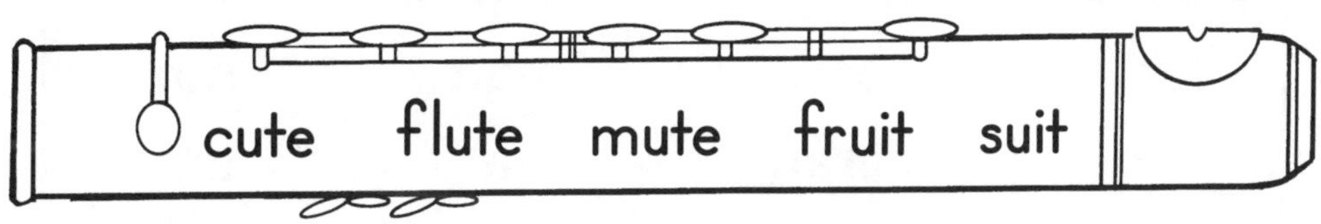

# Fan Word Search

**Directions:** Find and circle the "an" words in the puzzle.

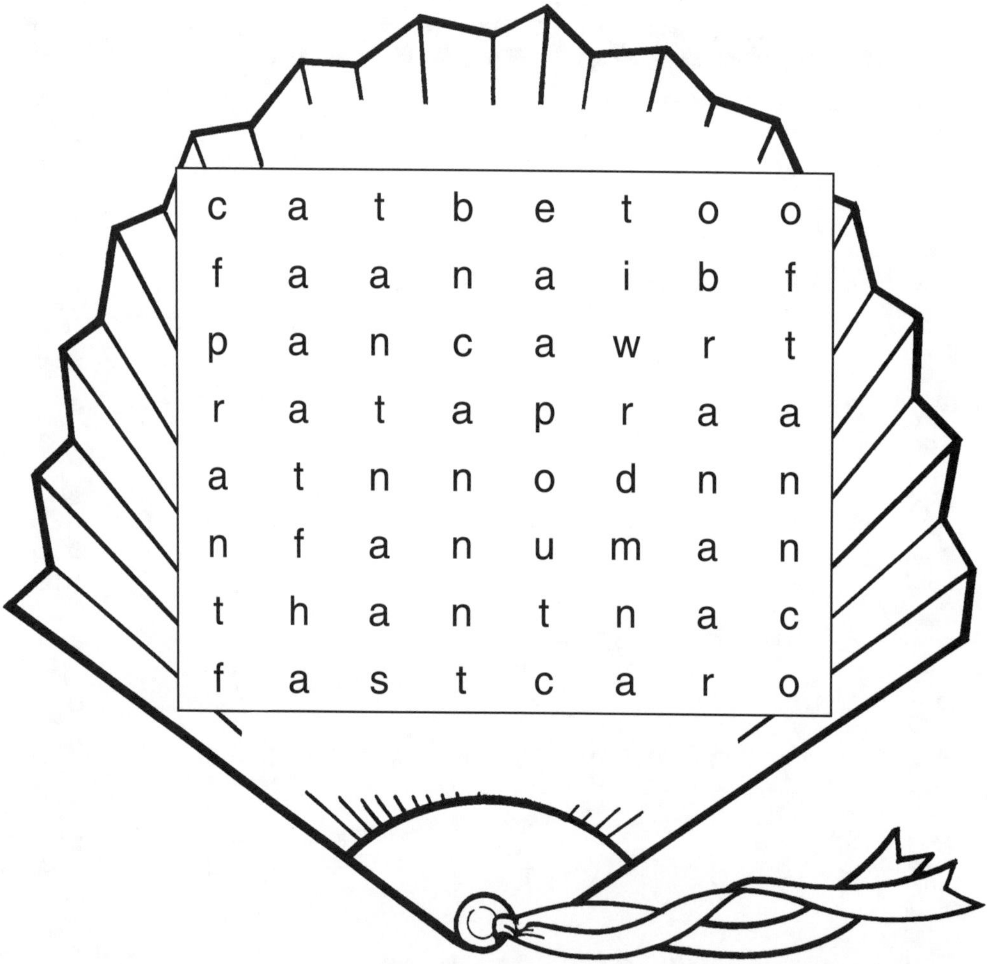

| | | | | | | | |
|---|---|---|---|---|---|---|---|
| c | a | t | b | e | t | o | o |
| f | a | a | n | a | i | b | f |
| p | a | n | c | a | w | r | t |
| r | a | t | a | p | r | a | a |
| a | t | n | n | o | d | n | n |
| n | f | a | n | u | m | a | n |
| t | h | a | n | t | n | a | c |
| f | a | s | t | c | a | r | o |

| | | | |
|---|---|---|---|
| **tan** | **pan** | **man** | **ran** |
| **can** | **bran** | **fan** | **than** |

# "ace" Words

**Directions:** Circle the words in the puzzle. Color the picture.

| | | | | | | | | | | | |
|---|---|---|---|---|---|---|---|---|---|---|---|
| k | d | g | w | e | o | f | h | f | e | w | a |
| a | p | c | a | l | a | r | a | c | e | d | c |
| w | l | a | e | t | r | a | c | e | g | n | e |
| s | a | l | h | w | e | k | s | f | r | j | l |
| s | c | p | a | r | b | s | p | a | c | e | d |
| m | e | m | e | l | a | c | e | c | d | s | u |
| q | g | r | a | c | e | g | o | e | f | k | b |

| | | | |
|---|---|---|---|
| ace | grace | place | space |
| face | lace | race | trace |

# "use" Words

**Directions:** Circle the words in the puzzle. Color the picture.

| | | | | | | | | | | |
|---|---|---|---|---|---|---|---|---|---|---|
| r | n | w | e | u | s | e | f | e | w | n |
| e | l | a | l | e | w | e | f | h | d | e |
| f | u | s | e | w | o | x | l | m | n | h |
| u | f | u | w | e | k | s | u | u | j | t |
| s | c | m | r | b | a | m | u | s | e | s |
| e | x | c | u | s | e | s | e | e | p | u |
| k | d | j | v | f | g | o | k | f | k | b |

| | | |
|---|---|---|
| fuse | use | excuse |
| muse | amuse | refuse |

# "ow" Words

**Directions:** Circle the words in the puzzle. Color the picture.

l m s a t e d y h b t
a o b l o w d e e r h
r a t t l e s s h o r
o t h e r g r o w k o
w a r n i n g l a e w
d i s h o w r d s n a
o l e o u i a m s o f
l o a n t n b o w t i
l w n e e d a w h a t

| | | | |
|---|---|---|---|
| blow | grow | mow | show |
| bow | low | row | throw |

# Hot Pot Search

**Directions:** Find and circle the "ot" words.

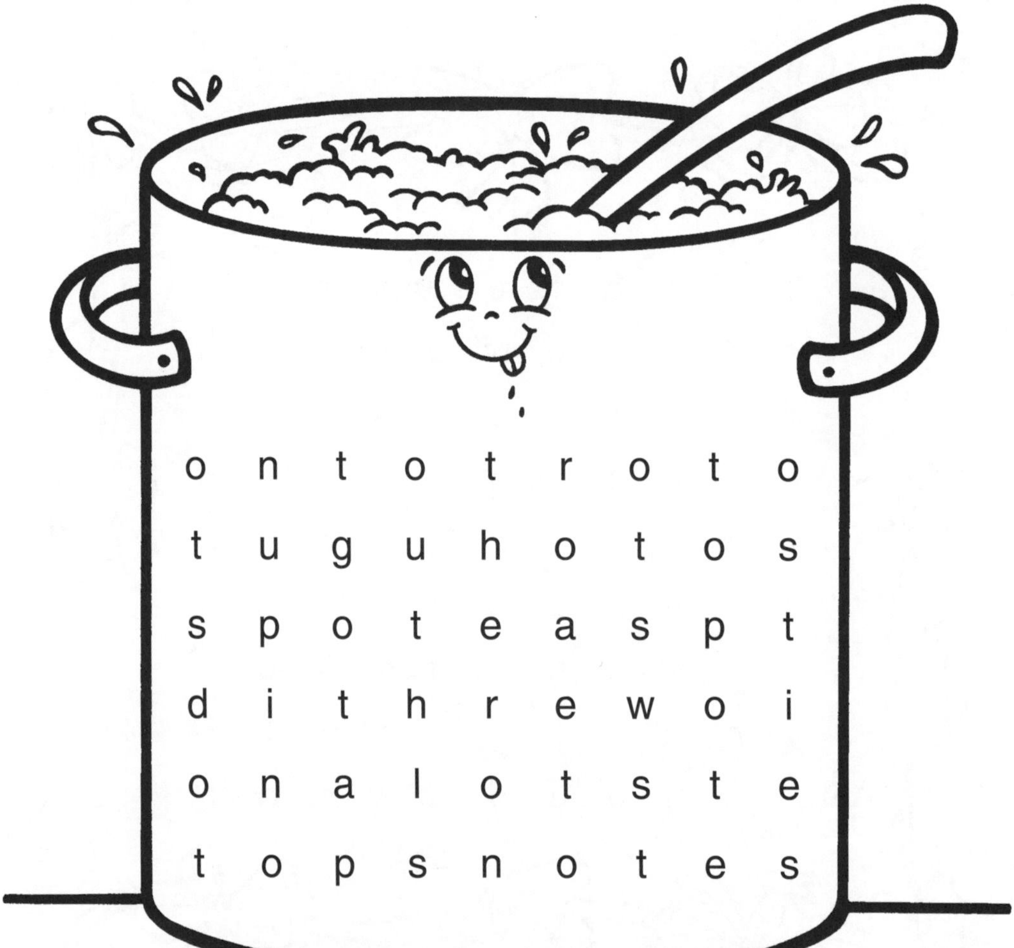

| | | | | | | | | |
|---|---|---|---|---|---|---|---|---|
| o | n | t | o | t | r | o | t | o |
| t | u | g | u | h | o | t | o | s |
| s | p | o | t | e | a | s | p | t |
| d | i | t | h | r | e | w | o | i |
| o | n | a | l | o | t | s | t | e |
| t | o | p | s | n | o | t | e | s |

| | | | |
|---|---|---|---|
| **trot** | **hot** | **lot** | **dot** |
| **spot** | **got** | **not** | **pot** |

# Swell Well Search

**Directions:** Find and circle the "ell" words.

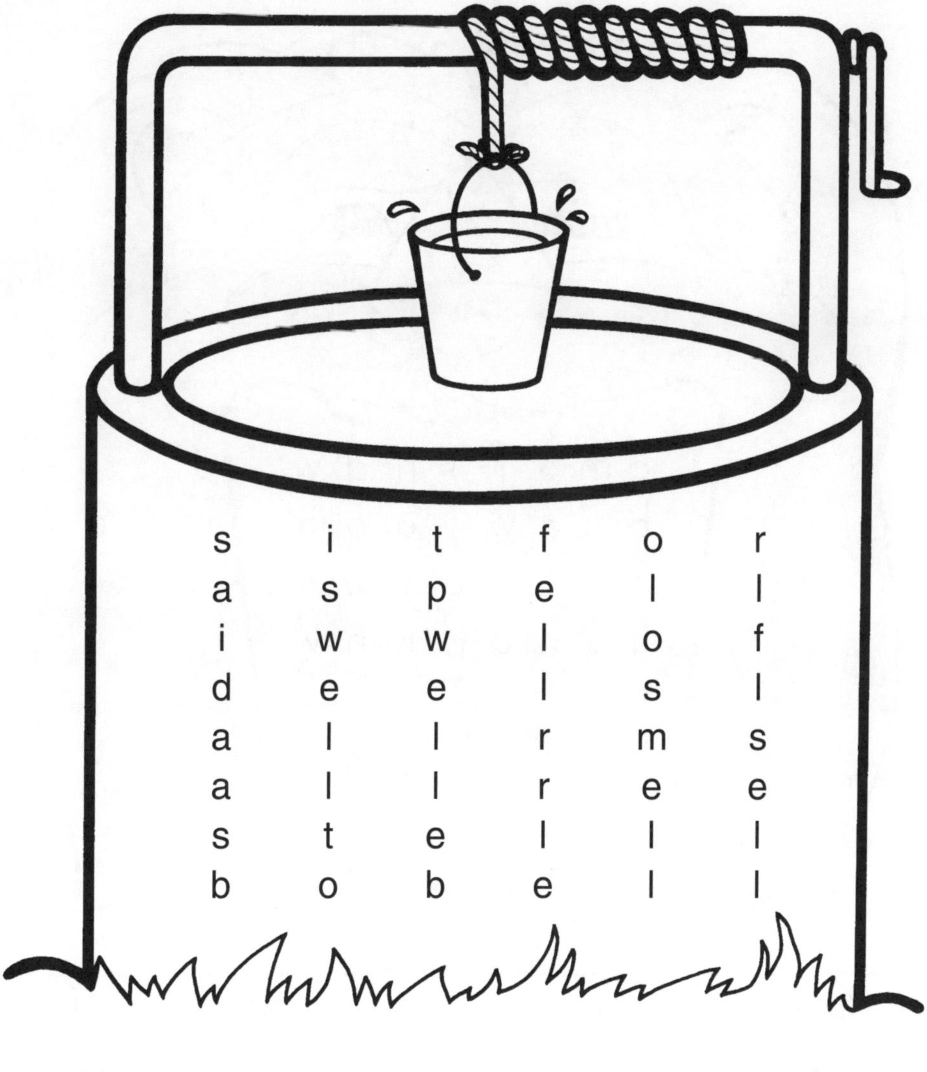

| s | i | t | f | o | r |
|---|---|---|---|---|---|
| a | s | p | e | l | l |
| i | w | w | l | o | f |
| d | e | e | l | s | l |
| a | l | l | r | m | s |
| a | l | l | r | e | e |
| s | t | e | l | l | l |
| b | o | b | e | l | l |

| | | | |
|---|---|---|---|
| **bell** | **well** | **fell** | **smell** |
| **tell** | **sell** | **spell** | **swell** |

# Sight Words

**Directions:** Leo is a strange lion. When he roars, only sight words come out! Find and circle the words across or down.

| | | | | | | | |
|---|---|---|---|---|---|---|---|
| a | m | o | f | i | n | d | w |
| b | a | r | w | l | o | o | h |
| o | n | t | h | a | t | w | o |
| u | y | h | a | d | h | n | w |
| t | o | e | t | i | e | o | i |
| b | u | i | o | d | y | w | t |
| u | r | r | o | o | n | e | h |

| | | | | |
|---|---|---|---|---|
| **their** | **what** | **they** | **now** | **or** |
| **that** | **who** | **many** | **did** | **find** |
| **down** | **with** | **you** | **one** | **too** |

GREAT
#1
YEAH!
COOL
WOW
NEAT
NEAT
GREAT
YEAH!
#1
GREAT
SUPER
WOW
YEAH!
#1
TOPS
SUPER
#1

#1
GREAT
YEAH!
WOW
GREAT
YEAH!
WOW
COOL
YEAH!
TOPS
TOPS
SUPER

# Scrambled Colors

**Directions:** Unscramble the color words. Then find them in the puzzle below.

**1.** der = ____________

**2.** lewylo = ___________

**3.** nerge = ____________

**4.** lcakb = ____________

**5.** ubel = ____________

**6.** lurppe = ___________

**7.** ageorn = ___________

**8.** thiwe = ____________

Words can be found going across, down, backwards, or upside-down.

| | | | | | | |
|---|---|---|---|---|---|---|
| N | E | E | R | G | P | C |
| J | U | A | B | L | U | W |
| B | L | A | C | K | R | O |
| C | B | R | E | D | P | L |
| E | T | I | H | W | L | L |
| O | R | A | N | G | E | E |
| R | D | S | T | O | H | Y |

# Circle the Number Words

**Directions:** Find the sum of the number pairs. Then circle the number words hidden in the letter maze. The words are written across. Example: 0 + 0 = 0

| | | | |
|---|---|---|---|
| 3 + 2 = ______ | 8 + 3 = ______ | 5 + 4 = ______ | 4 + 3 = ______ |
| 2 + 1 = ______ | 5 + 1 = ______ | 6 + 6 = ______ | 6 + 2 = ______ |
| 1 + 0 = ______ | 9 + 1 = ______ | 1 + 1 = ______ | 3 + 1 = ______ |

**zero**
**one**
**two**
**three**
**four**
**five**
**six**
**seven**
**eight**
**nine**
**ten**
**eleven**
**twelve**

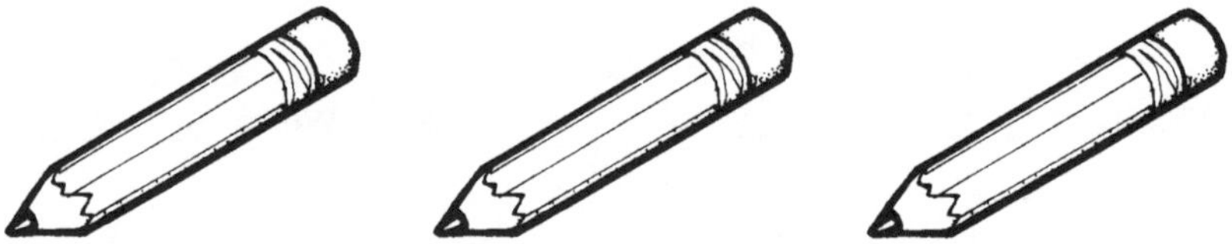

| | | | | | | | |
|---|---|---|---|---|---|---|---|
| s | e | v | e | n | o | n | e |
| w | e | l | e | v | e | n | z |
| l | v | t | w | e | l | v | e |
| t | e | n | i | n | e | s | i |
| f | o | u | r | z | e | r | o |
| e | i | g | h | t | w | o | g |
| l | f | i | v | e | s | i | x |
| h | t | h | r | e | e | f | n |

Ready·Set·Learn

# Short "U" Word Search

**Directions:** Write the name of each picture with the short "u" sound. Then, find and circle each word in the word search.

1.

_______________

2.

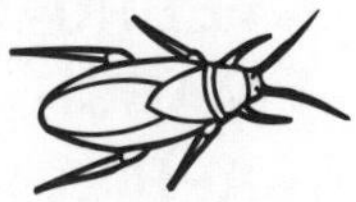

_______________

| S | U | N | R | S | B |
|---|---|---|---|---|---|
| J | L | T | U | M | U |
| U | T | U | G | U | G |
| G | U | B | V | G | N |
| L | G | E | B | U | N |
| R | U | N | O | K | P |
| G | R | C | W | H | D |
| D | O | F | S | U | B |
| C | U | B | L | G | C |

3.

_______________

4.

_______________

5.

_______________

6.

_______________

7.

_______________

8.

_______________

# Months

**Directions:** Look at the list of months. Find and circle those words in the puzzle below.

| | | |
|---|---|---|
| **JANUARY** | **MAY** | **SEPTEMBER** |
| **FEBRUARY** | **JUNE** | **OCTOBER** |
| **MARCH** | **JULY** | **NOVEMBER** |
| **APRIL** | **AUGUST** | **DECEMBER** |

| | | | | | | | | | |
|---|---|---|---|---|---|---|---|---|---|
| M | A | R | C | H | A | P | R | I | L |
| M | A | Y | O | C | T | O | B | E | R |
| C | W | D | E | C | E | M | B | E | R |
| W | J | U | L | Y | T | E | I | C | B |
| J | A | N | U | A | R | Y | Q | V | J |
| L | K | A | U | G | U | S | T | H | U |
| S | E | P | T | E | M | B | E | R | N |
| N | O | V | E | M | B | E | R | D | E |
| F | E | B | R | U | A | R | Y | T | I |

# Days of the Week

**Directions:** Look at the list of days. Find and circle those words in the puzzle below.

| | | |
|---|---|---|
| **SUNDAY** | **WEDNESDAY** | **FRIDAY** |
| **MONDAY** | **THURSDAY** | **SATURDAY** |
| **TUESDAY** | | |

| | | | | | | | | | |
|---|---|---|---|---|---|---|---|---|---|
| S | U | N | D | A | Y | A | X | H | H |
| V | S | A | T | O | R | F | A | Y | S |
| M | F | T | M | L | Y | R | C | P | A |
| T | P | O | J | D | F | I | U | N | T |
| W | E | D | N | E | S | D | A | Y | U |
| T | H | U | R | S | D | A | Y | Y | R |
| X | F | A | I | D | R | Y | S | H | D |
| T | U | E | S | D | A | Y | B | Z | A |
| D | M | O | N | D | A | Y | B | V | Y |

# Fruits and Vegetables

**Directions:** Look at the list of fruits and vegetables. Find and circle those words in the puzzle below.

| | | |
|---|---|---|
| **APPLES** | **CORN** | **PLUMS** |
| **CANTALOUPE** | **GRAPES** | **PUMPKINS** |
| **CARROTS** | **ORANGES** | **WATERMELON** |
| **CELERY** | **PEAS** | |

| | | | | | | | | | |
|---|---|---|---|---|---|---|---|---|---|
| V | A | P | P | L | E | S | A | J | C |
| O | R | A | N | G | E | S | R | B | A |
| W | A | T | E | R | M | E | L | O | N |
| G | R | A | P | E | S | X | H | N | T |
| P | P | U | M | P | K | I | N | S | A |
| E | M | F | L | E | N | T | U | C | L |
| A | P | L | U | M | S | M | L | Y | O |
| S | C | E | L | E | R | Y | P | K | U |
| P | O | J | D | F | C | O | R | N | P |
| U | N | C | A | R | R | O | T | S | E |

 

# Money

**Directions:** Look at the list of money words. Find and circle those words in the puzzle below.

| | | |
|---|---|---|
| **CENTS** | **DOLLAR** | **PENNY** |
| **CHANGE** | **MONEY** | **QUARTER** |
| **DIME** | **NICKEL** | **SAVE** |

| | | | | | | | | |
|---|---|---|---|---|---|---|---|---|
| S | P | Q | H | A | N | G | Q | E |
| N | I | C | K | E | L | P | U | M |
| Q | W | V | D | O | L | L | A | R |
| D | I | M | D | S | P | R | R | D |
| O | J | C | E | N | T | S | T | T |
| X | G | E | P | S | P | J | E | C |
| B | P | E | N | N | Y | R | R | D |
| U | A | R | T | N | R | O | H | I |
| W | W | C | H | A | N | G | E | M |
| M | O | N | E | Y | S | A | V | E |

# Animals

**Directions:** Look at the list of animals. Find and circle those words in the puzzle below.

**BEAR**
**CAT**
**DEER**
**DOVE**
**ELEPHANT**
**GIRAFFE**
**LION**
**MOUSE**
**RABBIT**

| D | O | V | E | R | A | B | L | A | T | N |
|---|---|---|---|---|---|---|---|---|---|---|
| B | A | A | R | G | L | M | O | U | S | E |
| E | O | G | A | F | I | I | H | C | A | L |
| R | L | I | E | W | O | R | O | O | N | E |
| A | D | R | E | P | N | X | A | N | F | P |
| B | M | A | D | E | E | R | U | F | L | H |
| B | O | F | L | H | F | A | A | C | F | A |
| I | R | F | B | E | A | R | N | A | A | N |
| T | S | E | D | I | I | N | N | T | G | T |

 

# Bugs

**Directions:** Look at the list of bugs. Find and circle those words in the puzzle below.

**ANT**
**BEE**
**BUTTERFLY**
**CRICKET**
**DRAGONFLY**

**FLY**
**LADYBUG**
**LOCUST**
**MOSQUITO**

| | | | | | | | | | |
|---|---|---|---|---|---|---|---|---|---|
| D | R | A | G | O | N | F | L | Y | R |
| L | O | C | U | S | T | L | L | Y | V |
| S | B | B | E | M | F | Y | M | L | Y |
| C | R | I | C | K | E | T | T | C | P |
| A | B | U | T | T | E | R | F | L | Y |
| T | N | Z | T | I | E | A | M | B | S |
| N | D | Y | D | X | S | N | L | E | Z |
| M | O | S | Q | U | I | T | O | E | D |
| W | L | A | D | Y | B | U | G | V | P |

# Telling Time

**Directions:** Look at the list of time words. Find and circle those words in the puzzle below.

| | |
|---|---|
| **CLOCK** | **MORNING** |
| **EVENING** | **SECOND** |
| **HANDS** | **TIME** |
| **HOUR** | **WATCH** |
| **MINUTE** | |

| | | | | | | | | | |
|---|---|---|---|---|---|---|---|---|---|
| M | O | R | N | I | N | G | E | C | W |
| E | V | E | N | I | N | G | W | T | E |
| C | C | B | Q | V | O | L | K | H | M |
| L | D | I | T | I | V | Y | M | O | H |
| O | D | B | C | L | O | C | I | U | N |
| C | O | U | R | P | Y | B | N | R | I |
| K | N | T | I | M | E | F | U | X | O |
| H | A | N | D | S | W | A | T | C | H |
| R | S | E | C | O | N | D | E | M | J |

# Shapes

**Directions:** Look at the list of shape words. Find and circle those words in the puzzle below.

| | |
|---|---|
| **CIRCLE** | **RECTANGLE** |
| **CORNERS** | **SHAPES** |
| **DIAMOND** | **SIDES** |
| **HEXAGON** | **SQUARE** |
| **OVAL** | **TRIANGLE** |

| C | I | R | C | L | E | U | D | O | W |
|---|---|---|---|---|---|---|---|---|---|
| D | I | A | M | O | N | D | X | O | S |
| S | R | Z | R | Z | O | M | B | V | S |
| H | E | X | A | G | O | N | I | A | H |
| A | C | T | R | I | A | N | G | L | E |
| P | O | C | O | R | N | E | R | S | T |
| E | R | E | C | T | A | N | G | L | E |
| S | S | Q | U | A | R | E | O | L | K |
| S | I | D | E | S | H | O | V | U | L |

# Plurals

**Directions:** Look at the list of words and their plurals. Find and circle those words in the puzzle below.

**BABY**
**BABIES**
**DADDY**
**DADDIES**
**LADY**
**LADIES**
**PUPPY**
**PUPPIES**
**STORY**
**STORIES**

| | | | | | | | | | | |
|---|---|---|---|---|---|---|---|---|---|---|
| S | P | U | P | P | I | E | S | T | B | D |
| T | J | W | L | F | L | W | F | G | A | A |
| O | Z | B | A | B | Y | N | L | C | B | D |
| R | P | G | D | D | C | D | Y | C | I | D |
| I | U | I | I | X | Y | K | L | Y | E | I |
| E | P | V | E | S | K | G | A | N | S | E |
| S | P | G | S | D | A | D | D | Y | P | S |
| R | Y | L | S | X | P | A | Y | P | U | O |
| F | J | A | T | K | U | S | T | O | R | Y |

# More Plurals

**Directions:** Look at the list of words and their plurals. Find and circle those words in the puzzle below.

**CANDY**
**CANDIES**
**CHERRY**
**CHERRIES**
**FRY**

**FRIES**
**PENNY**
**PENNIES**
**PONY**
**PONIES**

| F | Z | R | D | W | V | P | P | E | P | E |
|---|---|---|---|---|---|---|---|---|---|---|
| R | C | A | N | D | Y | E | M | E | O | N |
| Y | P | K | H | O | R | N | T | S | N | C |
| J | O | F | V | A | N | N | R | L | Y | H |
| X | N | R | O | I | M | Y | J | W | C | E |
| H | I | I | Z | H | T | O | F | T | H | R |
| N | E | E | X | A | Z | O | B | N | E | R |
| Q | S | S | C | H | E | R | R | Y | R | I |
| P | E | N | N | I | E | S | V | D | R | E |
| I | C | A | N | D | I | E | S | Y | I | S |

# Camping

**Directions:** Look at the list of camping words. Find and circle those words in the puzzle below.

| | |
|---|---|
| **CAMP** | **FOREST** |
| **CANOE** | **LANTERN** |
| **CRAFTS** | **STICK** |
| **FISHING** | **TENT** |
| **FIRE** | |

| | | | | | | | | | |
|---|---|---|---|---|---|---|---|---|---|
| C | A | M | P | C | A | N | O | E | H |
| S | T | I | C | K | P | R | V | S | M |
| F | F | O | R | E | S | T | T | M | L |
| L | A | N | T | E | R | N | Y | C | C |
| P | K | T | P | O | J | D | F | A | U |
| S | Z | T | F | I | S | H | I | N | G |
| T | E | R | M | B | S | N | R | O | D |
| C | R | A | F | T | S | T | E | N | T |

 

# Winter Word Search

**Directions:** Find and color the words in the word search. The words can be found horizontally, vertically, or diagonally.

| | | |
|---|---|---|
| **COLD** | **ESKIMO** | **HOT CHOCOLATE** |
| **ICE** | **IGLOO** | **JANUARY** |
| **JR** | **KING** | **LUTHER** |
| **MARTIN** | **MITTENS** | **PENGUIN** |
| **SKIS** | **SNOW** | **WINTER** |

| | | | | | | | | | | | |
|---|---|---|---|---|---|---|---|---|---|---|---|
| H | A | M | A | R | T | I | N | B | W | J | C |
| N | O | O | P | I | G | L | O | O | I | A | D |
| E | A | T | B | C | C | O | L | D | N | N | E |
| S | Z | S | C | M | L | M | N | O | T | U | L |
| K | Y | N | V | H | I | W | X | J | E | A | U |
| I | I | O | U | C | O | T | Y | R | R | R | T |
| M | K | W | K | B | D | C | T | P | D | Y | H |
| O | L | S | T | I | A | Z | O | E | E | Q | E |
| M | O | K | K | S | N | R | Q | L | N | R | R |
| L | O | J | I | I | H | G | G | F | A | S | F |
| I | C | E | X | W | S | V | U | T | S | T | G |
| K | J | P | E | N | G | U | I | N | I | H | E |

# I Only Have I's for You

**Directions:** Find the "I" words hidden in the word search puzzle. The words can be found down or across.

```
Q L K Q N J J Z X K Y K J P T Q G B F Y P Q
D Q H M N N N Z J S Y S K M N Y R M W D H R
    I H W F R C X V Z V F J G M B Y H Z
    G H T Y I H L T Q C W K M V W I S P
    U I L L C C X R V W W V Q Z W G X Y
    A K I Z I R J P T B I X M H J L W L
    N W S J C M B I Z P C V C I Y O F M
    A I D O L C P F I T E M G T R O R C
    M F Y P E C T J B S F X K L C M M S
    B Y N R J T H F P G Z X C Q M M Y N
    J P Z I J B I W D M B V Q F J P T H
    B N O N C V T E W X F T U I L M B V
    P L N T Y B M L P A A S D E U I O P
F J T L B O I R I S W Z Q M L G T T W V X W
Q J F G W S F V C G L K B Y S B Q Z G K W N
```

| | | |
|---|---|---|
| **IT** | **ILL** | **IF** |
| **ITEM** | **IGUANA** | **INTO** |
| **IGLOO** | **IRIS** | **IS** |
| **ICE** | **IDOL** | **ICICLE** |

# Words

**Directions:** Find the word "word" twenty times in the word search puzzle. It can be found across, down, or diagonally.

| | | | | | | | | | | | | | | | | | | |
|---|---|---|---|---|---|---|---|---|---|---|---|---|---|---|---|---|---|---|
| W | O | R | D | Z | Y | D | Z | W | O | R | D | Q | Z | B | W | S | V | Q |
| M | T | X | R | S | R | F | X | C | Q | G | P | L | R | T | W | O | R | D |
| G | T | S | X | O | V | C | C | W | L | T | G | M | W | H | O | B | Q | X |
| K | Y | B | W | Q | C | V | C | M | O | K | R | H | O | T | R | M | G | J |
| J | V | V | P | W | W | K | Y | T | Y | R | J | M | R | K | D | M | R | V |
| D | K | V | P | D | O | V | P | F | Q | F | D | W | D | V | T | G | R | D |
| Y | T | S | J | R | R | R | V | Z | R | Y | P | O | Z | G | Y | T | R | W |
| D | Z | W | Y | H | D | N | D | W | Y | W | O | R | D | B | G | O | F | O |
| J | Z | O | W | P | N | W | B | F | O | L | F | D | Y | L | W | M | G | R |
| W | O | R | D | D | M | V | T | J | T | R | L | L | Y | F | P | Y | X | D |
| T | C | D | X | F | Y | X | J | S | R | M | D | Q | Z | V | C | D | Z | Y |
| H | T | R | D | N | G | N | Y | R | W | B | P | V | P | C | Z | V | Y | W |
| T | P | W | W | Q | W | O | R | D | O | F | J | P | W | O | R | D | C | N |
| X | B | L | C | W | D | D | Q | S | R | M | S | J | T | R | R | B | V | Y |
| T | D | Y | J | S | K | K | K | Z | D | G | R | B | F | O | Z | X | V | C |
| B | V | R | S | W | Y | C | D | T | Q | Y | N | G | W | N | V | W | G | D |

# It's About Time

| G | P | D | R | T | W | E | H | T | E | H | A |
|---|---|---|---|---|---|---|---|---|---|---|---|
| C | N | M | I | A | H | C | O | T | L | F | G |
| L | R | I | T | N | N | G | U | B | T | R | N |
| O | S | C | N | U | N | N | I | E | R | Y | I |
| C | H | L | L | R | I | E | R | N | Q | L | N |
| K | M | V | E | M | O | N | R | L | L | R | E |
| A | W | A | K | E | O | M | R | A | L | A | V |
| Y | A | D | A | O | P | T | T | B | H | E | E |
| Q | V | I | N | O | Y | E | X | I | O | D | W |
| T | S | A | F | K | A | E | R | B | U | O | J |
| G | B | Q | S | E | C | O | N | D | R | M | D |

**Directions:** Find these words about time in the puzzle.

**AFTERNOON**
**ALARM**
**AWAKE**

**BREAKFAST**
**CLOCK**
**DAY**
**DINNER**
**EARLY**
**EVENING**
**HOUR**

**LATE**
**LUNCH**
**MINUTE**
**MORNING**
**NIGHT**
**SECOND**
**SLEEP**
**WATCH**

Ready·Set·Learn

# What's for Breakfast?

| B | O | R | A | N | G | E | J | U | I | C | E | L | L |
|---|---|---|---|---|---|---|---|---|---|---|---|---|---|
| O | W | R | F | R | E | M | U | F | F | I | N | L | W |
| A | E | L | F | R | H | S | N | E | R | F | O | H | H |
| S | G | G | E | D | E | L | B | M | A | R | C | S | E |
| T | S | P | A | G | O | N | E | A | N | C | B | B | A |
| A | I | J | A | S | A | J | C | O | C | N | B | K | T |
| U | E | U | U | N | U | B | M | H | A | O | E | L | T |
| S | O | T | R | I | C | A | N | X | T | G | N | I | O |
| A | M | A | H | F | N | A | E | M | A | O | U | M | A |
| G | E | R | A | N | H | E | K | S | T | C | A | H | S |
| H | N | C | I | G | E | S | U | E | S | O | N | S | T |
| E | E | C | J | E | J | A | E | I | S | O | W | S | T |
| N | T | E | H | A | S | H | B | R | O | W | N | S | T |
| K | L | O | M | L | F | E | L | F | F | A | W | S | T |

**Directions:** How many of these have you eaten for breakfast? Find their names in the puzzle.

**BACON**
**BAGEL**
**BISCUIT**
**CINNAMON ROLL**
**FRENCH TOAST**
**FRESH FRUIT**
**HAM**
**HASH BROWNS**
**MILK**
**MUFFIN**
**ORANGE JUICE**
**PANCAKES**
**SAUSAGE**
**SCRAMBLED EGGS**
**WAFFLE**
**WHEAT TOAST**

# Hamburger Helpers

| | | | | | | | | | | | | |
|---|---|---|---|---|---|---|---|---|---|---|---|---|
| K | E | T | A | H | B | B | H | E | S | E | Q | E |
| E | S | C | O | T | A | M | O | T | J | L | X | C |
| T | E | S | O | C | R | D | S | J | Q | P | N | U |
| C | E | V | O | L | B | R | G | H | Z | P | M | T |
| H | H | N | H | N | E | S | A | L | S | A | P | T |
| U | C | K | O | P | C | S | K | A | Y | E | I | E |
| P | F | I | P | U | U | D | L | O | J | N | C | L |
| F | N | E | P | L | E | S | N | A | U | I | K | I |
| O | P | W | T | A | S | N | S | O | W | P | L | G |
| S | E | L | O | M | A | C | A | U | G | F | E | T |
| C | H | I | L | I | U | D | R | A | T | S | U | M |
| D | H | I | S | K | C | R | E | L | I | S | H | M |
| J | U | E | C | T | E | R | I | Y | A | K | I | T |

**Directions:** In the puzzle, find these 18 things you can put on a hamburger.

**BACON**
**BARBECUE SAUCE**
**CHEESE**
**CHILI**
**COLESLAW**
**GUACAMOLE**
**KETCHUP**
**LETTUCE**
**MAYONNAISE**
**MUSTARD**
**ONION**
**PEPPERS**
**PICKLE**
**PINEAPPLE**
**RELISH**
**SALSA**
**TERIYAKI**
**TOMATO**

# Pizza Toppings

**Directions:** Find these pizza toppings in the puzzle.

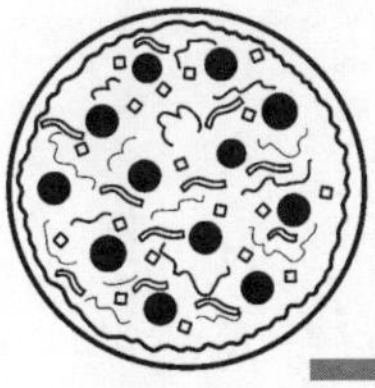

| | | | | | | | | | | | | |
|---|---|---|---|---|---|---|---|---|---|---|---|---|
| F | P | H | T | J | L | D | O | H | B | V | X | U |
| F | C | S | O | F | J | P | I | M | A | H | I | U |
| L | M | R | M | S | R | S | W | F | C | D | M | G |
| U | I | E | A | O | O | S | E | I | O | A | A | Q |
| O | U | P | T | W | O | E | I | V | N | P | L | S |
| R | N | P | O | S | B | R | I | C | I | O | A | Q |
| L | A | E | S | V | A | L | H | N | S | L | S | N |
| C | H | P | A | G | I | O | E | S | D | A | O | M |
| E | H | Q | U | H | V | A | Q | D | U | T | K | W |
| J | Q | E | C | Y | P | V | V | S | E | M | A | F |
| W | T | I | E | P | T | N | A | L | P | G | G | E |
| E | S | A | L | S | A | G | E | G | R | T | O | B |
| A | P | E | P | P | E | R | O | N | I | O | N | S |

| | | |
|---|---|---|
| **ANCHOVY** | **GARLIC** | **PEPPERS** |
| **BACON** | **HAM** | **PINEAPPLE** |
| **BEEF** | **MUSHROOMS** | **SALAMI** |
| **CHEESE** | **OLIVES** | **SALSA** |
| **CHILI** | **ONIONS** | **SAUSAGE** |
| **EGGPLANT** | **PEPPERONI** | **TOMATO SAUCE** |

# Musical Instruments

| X | T | S | F | Q | D | R | P | C | T | P | I |
|---|---|---|---|---|---|---|---|---|---|---|---|
| T | A | E | O | L | A | U | L | N | E | I | P |
| M | K | A | P | T | U | A | I | L | N | A | A |
| S | T | V | I | M | R | T | J | M | R | N | H |
| E | A | U | G | I | U | C | E | G | O | O | A |
| B | G | X | N | G | M | R | G | R | C | T | R |
| D | B | E | O | K | M | P | T | F | O | F | M |
| W | T | Z | N | P | V | I | O | L | I | N | O |
| U | E | E | X | Z | H | M | U | R | D | R | N |
| U | E | N | O | B | M | O | R | T | G | J | I |
| T | F | U | G | W | X | C | N | A | T | O | C |
| P | B | E | P | M | I | Q | N | E | P | L | A |

**Directions:** Find the names of all these instruments in the puzzle above.

**CLARINET**
**CORNET**
**DRUM**
**FLUTE**
**GUITAR**
**HARMONICA**
**ORGAN**
**PIANO**
**SAXOPHONE**
**TROMBONE**
**TRUMPET**
**VIOLIN**

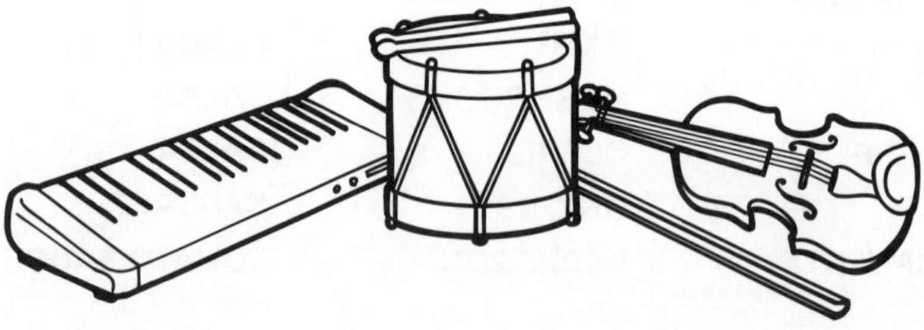

Ready·Set·Learn

# Directions

| N | E | A | R | U | E | T | T | V | F | B | D |
|---|---|---|---|---|---|---|---|---|---|---|---|
| T | N | O | P | U | H | R | D | S | E | Z | N |
| N | H | H | T | R | O | N | O | Y | E | R | U |
| W | M | E | O | N | I | I | O | F | L | W | O |
| O | B | U | R | H | I | N | W | O | E | L | R |
| D | G | E | E | E | D | S | H | A | V | B | A |
| H | U | B | S | W | T | I | K | T | J | E | F |
| S | N | G | O | I | I | D | W | V | U | V | R |
| K | D | L | V | V | D | E | Y | I | J | O | I |
| C | E | B | A | F | T | E | R | U | Q | B | S |
| B | R | V | E | D | I | S | T | U | O | A | B |
| A | C | R | O | S | S | T | S | A | E | I | K |

**Directions:** Find these direction words in the puzzle.

**ABOVE**
**ACROSS**
**AFTER**
**AROUND**
**BEFORE**
**BEHIND**
**BELOW**
**BESIDE**

**BEYOND**
**DOWN**
**EAST**
**FAR**
**INSIDE**
**INTO**
**NEAR**
**NORTH**

**OUTSIDE**
**OVER**
**SOUTH**
**THERE**
**THROUGH**
**UNDER**
**UPON**
**WEST**

# Call It Art

| V | T | W | U | B | F | H | Z | D | J | P | Y | C | G | F |
|---|---|---|---|---|---|---|---|---|---|---|---|---|---|---|
| M | Y | R | Z | K | F | A | O | W | R | F | R | O | W | U |
| O | I | L | P | A | I | N | T | I | N | G | L | M | N | R |
| D | A | N | C | E | S | U | N | T | E | K | E | P | R | N |
| F | P | V | O | C | I | T | H | R | H | R | W | U | O | I |
| I | Y | H | I | B | M | E | U | N | U | U | E | T | L | T |
| L | L | M | O | A | A | T | M | T | W | H | J | E | O | U |
| M | O | H | K | T | A | N | C | U | V | D | J | R | C | R |
| C | K | I | E | R | O | E | O | L | S | B | O | A | R | E |
| A | N | R | E | X | T | G | A | I | Y | I | G | R | E | I |
| G | M | T | R | I | D | W | R | W | H | W | C | T | T | P |
| O | I | T | H | G | N | I | P | A | C | S | D | N | A | L |
| L | N | C | A | I | F | X | X | A | P | R | A | I | W | N |
| Q | R | G | N | I | W | A | R | D | V | H | D | F | H | Y |
| A | S | C | U | L | P | T | U | R | E | D | Y | U | C | L |

**Directions:** Art comes in many forms. Find these different kinds of art in the puzzle.

**ARCHITECTURE**
**COMICS**
**COMPUTER ART**
**DANCE**
**DRAWING**
**FASHION**
**FILM**
**FURNITURE**
**JEWELRY**
**LANDSCAPING**
**LITERATURE**
**MUSIC**
**OIL PAINTING**
**PHOTOGRAPHY**
**PRINTMAKING**
**SCULPTURE**
**THEATER**
**WATERCOLOR**

# Team Sports

| W | R | E | S | T | L | I | N | G | O | R | T | F |
|---|---|---|---|---|---|---|---|---|---|---|---|---|
| B | I | E | L | U | S | R | G | L | L | B | E | O |
| L | T | C | Y | L | U | O | O | C | A | U | A | O |
| L | E | S | E | G | A | P | C | S | S | L | M | T |
| A | N | M | B | H | R | B | E | C | L | W | H | B |
| B | N | Y | A | E | O | B | T | A | E | M | A | A |
| Y | I | F | T | U | A | C | B | E | C | R | N | L |
| E | S | A | T | L | C | T | K | E | K | D | D | L |
| L | W | L | L | T | F | F | E | E | C | S | B | Y |
| L | E | S | S | O | R | C | A | L | Y | U | A | N |
| O | G | D | S | C | R | I | C | K | E | T | L | B |
| V | O | L | O | P | I | O | H | Q | H | V | L | I |
| Y | E | K | C | O | H | R | E | L | L | O | R | J |

**Directions:** Find and circle these sports in the puzzle.

**BASEBALL**
**BASKETBALL**
**CRICKET**
**FOOTBALL**
**ICE HOCKEY**
**LACROSSE**
**POLO**
**ROLLER HOCKEY**
**RUGBY**
**SOCCER**
**SOFTBALL**
**TEAM HANDBALL**
**TENNIS**
**VOLLEYBALL**
**WATER POLO**
**WRESTLING**

# Answer Key

**Page 4**

l f a s m o g
i r s t l n d
h o g e o d o
i g g e g j d
f o g r o o o
e s c l o g g
e e m e s i n

**Page 5**

s o g g y o w e t
t g o p e n u p h
o e t e s e t b e
r t o t h e j e t
m e t m e l e t y

**Page 6**

s p u n o m u g
u l n d u g r u
b u g a g s u m
u g b y h u g e
n s i s t n j e
r a t u g h u t
a d e n o t g o

**Page 7**

t o s p i n i b
h e a t t i n y
i f g r i n g p
n o p i n o f i
g r i p o w i n
o c h i n a n g
f r o g e y e s

**Page 8**

j s u m v u n o p
u t u b l a s f u
s u n o n e p l m
t n u t o r u n p
a o b u n a n u t
n r u b i n f u n

**Page 9**

z f w t c o l d
a r i o a l a p
p m a p p n p c
e i n t r a p l
u z a e x v r a
i o p t a p w p

**Page 10**

m d n w b a k e f e w r
a b l a k e w e m h d a
n w k e j w a x r c n k
j a k e e e k s c a j e
s m a k e b e d a k s d
m a m n b x t a k e w u

**Page 11**

s p i c e b f d w i s d
a n l p r i c e n h e e
d i c e j w e x r i c e
s c m h w c k s i c o w
k e i c i c e h f p r n
m z c n b x n s l d p u
q k e j v f t w i c e b

**Page 12**

s p o t b k m
w i d h e i r
n t o e s t i
s l i t s t i
g s f i t e p
i b a s i t p
h i t l i t e
e t r o b e d

**Page 13**

z z i p p e r y t i n
i o s u m m e r r s o
s i p f d o s h i p d
g i r l i p t i p o o
e m h i p l a r i p s
r i m p e l y l m e e

**Page 14**

f h m e k m i r j w
d b r g f e e i s e
t e b x n s t d s d
c r e t f h r q w s
l a e a p e e d o e
a u h w o x e g n e
b t m h g o k h o n

**Page 15**

b e e p r b f d w i s d
m s m n b x n e l d w u
k h k e e p f e f e e p
a e l a e a w p m h e e
n e a n j e e p r g p e
q p k j v f g o w e e p

# Answer Key *(cont.)*

### Page 16

```
b o g e g j o t
a n a m e o c e
g p h o t g z c
o g o t e t o o
s a g n o f g g
f o g a p o o o
g l o c t r l m
f r o g e g o s
d o g o w g g o
```

### Page 20

```
d f h w h e a t r j
d t r e a t h f e r
t m e j w o e r a n
m d n r b m a t i e
z r e a t e t l d a
k d h v f a o k f t
s e a t a t b e a t
```

### Page 24

```
k s n w e t i g h t w n
b s i g h t f e b h d i
r w l u j w i x r g n g
i r i g p t g s i m j h
g m g n r t h d g r s t
h z h n b x t s h b s u
t k t f m i g h t m k b
```

### Page 17

```
o w v e s t h e m
v e e r t o m a a
e s n b o n e s t
r t t e l l y t e
c h e s t y e i s
o l d t o r e s t
b u m p e s t h o
```

### Page 21

```
b b n w e o h o l d w n
a o l a l a w e m h d d
s l m e j c o o f g n t
o d f d w o o l o r j o
l m d n r l f d l i s l
d z m n r d n s d d s d
q g o l d f g o k f k b
```

### Page 25

```
s d s u i t k s i r f w
s m d e r b f t i o r f
m z x n b x l s l d u u
k u n w e o u h f e i n
c u t e l a t e m h t e
n w a e j w e x r g n d
q k d j v f g o m u t e
```

### Page 18

```
b o a t t r i p
l n r o c k s k
o f s o c k h n
c l o c k l o o
k c o p l o c c
l o t s h c k k
d o c k s k i l
```

### Page 22

```
d u s t b r u s t m
o g t r u n a m o u
t h r u s t p a n s
g r i m t r u s t t
u m p j u s t t s s
s u s d w c a t e v
t e e t e r t e n n
```

### Page 26

```
c a t b e t o o
f a a n a i b f
p a n c a w r t
r a t a p r a a
a t n n o d n n
n f a n u m a n
t h a n t n a c
f a s t c a r o
```

### Page 19

```
w w a f i n e x r g n d
i s l a p n w p i n e s
n d f n w e k d i n e h
e m i n e b f d w i s i
m h m v b x b s l d s n
s d n w e o l i n e w e
q k v i n e g o k f k b
```

### Page 23

```
q j o k e f g y k f k c
s p f h w s k o i r j h
e s o a l m w k b h e o
s w a l h o o e r g k k
o m d n e k f d o i o e
w o k e b e p o k e r u
k s p o k e f h e e w n
```

### Page 27

```
k d g w e o f h f e w a
a p c a l a r a c e d c
w l a e t r a c e g n e
s a l h w e k s f r j l
s c p a r b s p a c e d
m e m e l a c e c d s u
q g r a c e g o e f k b
```

# Answer Key *(cont.)*

**Page 28**

```
r n w e u s e f e w n
e l a l e w e f h d e
f u s e w o x l m n h
u f u w e k s u u j t
s c m r b a m u s e s
e x c u s e s e e p u
k d j v f g o k f k b
```

**Page 29**

```
l m s a t e d y h b t
a o b l o w d e e r h
r a t t l e s s h o r
o t h e r g r o w k o
w a r n i n g l a e w
d i s h o w r d s n a
o l e o u i a m s o f
l o a n t n b o w t i
l w n e e d a w h a t
```

**Page 30**

```
o n t o t r o t o
t u g u h o t o s
s p o t e a s p t
d i t h r e w o i
o n a l o t s t e
t o p s n o t e s
```

**Page 31**

```
s i t f o r
a s p e l l
i w w l o f
d e e l s l
a l l r m s
a l l r e e
s t e l l l
b o b e l l
```

**Page 32**

```
a m o f i n d w
b a r w l o o h
o n t h a t w o
u y h a d h n w
t o e t i e o i
b u i o d y w t
u r r o o n e h
```

**Page 33**

```
N E E R G P C
J U A B L U W
B L A C K R O
C B R E D P L
E T I H W L L
O R A N G E E
R D S T O H Y
```

**Page 34**

```
s e v e n o n e
w e l e v e n z
l v t w e l v e
t e n i n e s i
f o u r z e r o
e i g h t w o g
l f i v e s i x
h t h r e e f n
```

**Page 35**

```
S U N R S B
J L T U M U
U T U G U G
G U B V G N
L G E B U N
R U N O K P
G R C W H D
D O F S U B
C U B L G C
```

**Page 36**

```
M A R C H A P R I L
M A Y O C T O B E R
C W D E C E M B E R
W J U L Y T E I C B
J A N U A R Y Q V J
L K A U G U S T H U
S E P T E M B E R N
N O V E M B E R D E
F E B R U A R Y T I
```

**Page 37**

```
S U N D A Y A X H H
V S A T O R F A Y S
M F T M L Y R C P A
T P O J D F I U N T
W E D N E S D A Y U
T H U R S D A Y Y R
X F A I D R Y S H D
T U E S D A Y B Z A
D M O N D A Y B V Y
```

**Page 38**

```
V A P P L E S A J C
O R A N G E S R B A
W A T E R M E L O N
G R A P E S X H N T
P P U M P K I N S A
E M F L E N T U C L
A P L U M S M L Y O
S C E L E R Y P K U
P O J D F C O R N P
U N C A R R O T S E
```

**Page 39**

```
S P Q H A N G Q E
N I C K E L P U M
Q W V D O L L A R
D I M D S P R R D
O J C E N T S T T
X G E P S P J E C
B P E N N Y R R D
U A R T N R O H I
W W C H A N G E M
M O N E Y S A V E
```

# Answer Key *(cont.)*

**Page 40**

D O V E R A B L A T N
B A A R G L M O U S E
E O G A F I I H C A L
R L I E W O R O O N E
A D R E P N X A N F P
B M A D E E R U F L H
B O F L H F A A C F A
I R F B E A R N A A N
T S E D I I N N T G T

**Page 41**

D R A G O N F L Y R
L O C U S T L L Y V
S B B E M F Y M L Y
C R I C K E T T C P
A B U T T E R F L Y
T N Z T I E A M B S
N D Y D X S N L E Z
M O S Q U I T O E D
W L A D Y B U G V P

**Page 42**

M O R N I N G E C W
E V E N I N G W T E
C C B Q V O L K H M
L D I T I V Y M O H
O D B C L O C I U N
C O U R P Y B N R I
K N T I M E F U X O
H A N D S W A T C H
R S E C O N D E M J

**Page 43**

C I R C L E U D O W
D I A M O N D X O S
S R Z R Z O M B V S
H E X A G O N I A H
A C T R I A N G L E
P O C O R N E R S T
E R E C T A N G L E
S S Q U A R E O L K
S I D E S H O V U L

**Page 44**

S P U P P I E S T B D
T J W L F L W F G A A
O Z B A B Y N L C B D
R P G D D C D Y C I D
I U I I X Y K L Y E I
E P V E S K G A N S E
S P G S D A D D Y P S
R Y L S X P A Y P U O
F J A T K U S T O R Y

**Page 45**

F Z R D W V P P E P E
R C A N D Y E M E O N
Y P K H O R N T S N C
J O F V A N N R L Y H
X N R O I M Y J W C E
H I I Z H T O F T H R
N E E X A Z O B N E R
Q S S C H E R R Y R I
P E N N I E S V D R E
I C A N D I E S Y I S

**Page 46**

C A M P C A N O E H
S T I C K P R V S M
F F O R E S T T M L
L A N T E R N Y C C
P K T P O J D F A U
S Z T F I S H I N G
T E R M B S N R O D
C R A F T S T E N T

**Page 47**

H A M A R T I N B W J C
N O O P I G L O O I A D
E A T B C C O L D N N E
S Z S C M L M N O T U L
K Y N V H I W X J E A U
I I O U C O T Y R R R T
M K W K B D C T P D Y H
O L S T I A Z O E E Q E
M O K K S N R Q L N R R
L O J I I H G G F A S F
I C E X W S V U T S T G
K J P E N G U I N I H E

**Page 48**

Q L K Q N J J Z X K Y K J P T Q G B F Y P Q
D Q H M N N N Z J S Y S K M N Y R M W D H R
I H W F R C X V Z V F J G M B Y H Z
G H T Y I H L T Q C W K M V W I S P
U I L L C C X R V W W V Q Z W G X Y
A K I Z I R J P T B I X M H J L W L
N W S J C M B I Z P C V C I Y O F M
A I D O L C P F I T E M G T R O R C
M F Y P E C T J B S F X K L C M M S
B Y N R J T H F P G Z X C Q M M Y N
J P Z I J B I W D M B V Q F J P T H
B N O N C V T E W X F T U I L M B V
P L N T Y B M L P A A S D E U I O P
F J T L B O I R I S W Z Q M L G T T W V X W
Q J F G W S F V C G L K B Y S B Q Z G K W N

**Page 49**

W O R D Z Y D Z W O R D Q Z B W S V Q
M T X R S R F X C Q G P L R T W O R D
G T S X O V C C W L T G M W H O B Q X
K Y B W Q C V C M O K R H O T R M G J
J V V P W W K Y T Y R J M R K D M R V
D K V P D O V P F Q F D W D V T G R D
Y T S J H R R V Z R Y P O Z G Y T R W
D Z W Y H D N D W Y W O R D B G O F O
J Z O W P N W B F O L F D Y L W M G R
W O R D D M V T J T R L L Y F P Y X D
T C D X F Y X J S R M D Q Z V C D Z Y
H T R D N G N Y R W B P V P C Z V Y W
T P W W Q W O R D O F J P W O R D C N
X B L C W D D Q S R M S J T R R B V Y
T D Y J S K K K Z D G R B F O Z X V C
B V R S W Y C D T Q Y N G W N V W G D

**Page 50**

G P D R T W E H T E H A
C N M I A H C O T L F G
L R I T N N G U B T R N
O S C N U N N I E R Y I
C H L L R I E R N Q L N
K M V E M O N R L L R E
A W A K E O M R A L A V
Y A D A O P T T B H E E
Q V I N O Y E X I O D W
T S A F K A E R B U O J
G B Q S E C O N D R M D

**Page 51**

B O R A N G E J U I C E L L
O W R F R E M U F F I N L W
A E L F R H S N E R F O H H
S G G E D E L B M A R C S E
T S P A G O N E A N C B B A
A I J A S A J C O C N B K T
U E U U N U B M H A O E L T
S O T R I C A N X T G N I O
A M A H F N A E M A O U M A
G E R A N H E K S T C A H S
H N C I G E S U E S O N S T
E E C J E J A E I S O W S T
N T E H A S H B R O W N S T
K L O M L F E L F F A W S T

# Answer Key *(cont.)*

**Page 52**

```
K E T A H B B H E S E Q E
E S C O T A M O T J L X C
T E S O C R D S J Q P N U
C E V O L B R G H Z P M T
H H N H N E S A L S A P T
U C K O P C S K A Y E I E
P F I P U U D L O J N C L
F N E P L E S N A U I K I
O P W T A S N S O W P L G
S E L O M A C A U G F E T
C H I L I U D R A T S U M
D H I S K C R E L I S H M
J U E C T E R I Y A K I T
```

**Page 54**

```
X T S F Q D R P C T P I
T A E O L A U L N E I P
M K A P T U A I L N A A
S T V I M R T J M R N H
E A U G I U C E G O O A
B G X N G M R G R C T R
D B E O K M P T F O F M
W T Z N P V I O L I N O
U E E X Z H M U R D R N
U E N O B M O R T G J I
T F U G W X C N A T O C
P B E P M I Q N E P L A
```

**Page 56**

```
V T W U B F H Z D J P Y C G F
M Y R Z K F A O W R F R O W U
O I L P A I N T I N G L M N R
D A N C E S U N T E K E P R N
F P V O C I T H R H R W U O I
I Y H I B M E U N U U E T L T
L L M O A A T M T W H J E O U
M O H K T A N C U V D J R C R
C K I E R O E O L S B O A R E
A N R E X T G A I Y I G R E I
G M T R I D W R W H W C T T P
O I T H G N I P A C S D N A L
L N C A I F X X A P R A I W N
Q R G N I W A R D V H D F H Y
A S C U L P T U R E D Y U C L
```

**Page 53**

```
F P H T J L D O H B V X U
F C S O F J P I M A H I U
L M R M S R S W F C D M G
U I E A O O S E I O A A Q
O U P T W O E L V N P L S
R N P O S B R I C I O A Q
L A E S V A L H N S L S N
C H P A G I O E S D A O M
E H Q U H V A Q D U T K W
J Q E C Y P V V S E M A F
W T I E P T N A L P G G E
E S A L S A G E G R T O B
A P E P P E R O N I O N S
```

**Page 55**

```
N E A R U E T T V F B D
T N O P U H R D S E Z N
N H H T R O N O Y E R U
W M E O N I I O F L W O
O B U R H I N W O E L R
D G E E E D S H A V B A
H U B S W T I K T J E F
S N G O I I D W V U V R
K D L V V D E Y I J O I
C E B A F T E R U Q B S
B R V E D I S T U O A B
A C R O S S T S A E I K
```

**Page 57**

```
W R E S T L I N G O R T F
B I E L U S R G L L B E O
L T C Y L U O O C A U A O
L E S E G A P C S S L M T
A N M B H R B E C L W H B
B N Y A E O B T A E M A A
Y I F T U A C B E C R N L
E S A T L C T K E K D D L
L W L L T F F E E C S B Y
L E S S O R C A L Y U A N
O G D S C R I C K E T L B
V O L O P I O H Q H V L I
Y E K C O H R E L L O R J
```

# This Award Is Presented To

________________________________________

for

- ★ Doing Your Best
- ★ Trying Hard
- ★ Not Giving Up
- ★ Making a Great Effort